Chinese Quick Guides

CHINESE ETIQUETT
AND CULTURE

Cathy Xiaoxia Zhou

LONG RIVER PRESS
San Francisco

Author: Cathy Xiaoxia Zhou

Edition Editor: Lily Lijuan Zhou

Cover Design & Layout: SinoMedia Ltd.

Illustrations: Fu Jie

Publisher: Zhang Ruizhi & Xu Mingqiang

First Edition July 2005

ISBN 1-59265-044-9

Published in the United States of America by

Long River Press

360 Swift Ave., Suite 48, South San Francisco, CA 94080

www.longriverpress.com

in association with Haiwen Audio-Video Publishers

Printed in China

Introduction

With the advance of modern technology and communications, the world feels smaller. The technical improvements have made the once formidable geographical distance accessible. Peoples of different cultures find themselves interacting more closely than ever. Physical distance is no longer an obstacle preventing the interaction, but understanding of cultures different from one's own emerges as a new challenge.

This book, as its title shows, aims at, from a cultural perspective, providing some tips to those who are working or living in China and who want to make friends with the Chinese. The Chinese culture, with its evolution for over five thousand years, has formed its unique characteristics and has exerted a tremendous influence on all of Asia. The questions such as how and why the Chinese behave as they do require a careful probing of their cultural background. If we think of Chinese culture as a huge tree, then this book may be like some leaves which might enable you to imagine the tree from which they come. Generally speaking, the Chinese take a pragmatic attitude toward life, which can be seen in their interpersonal relationships and also their various holidays and celebrations. The author is concerned with understanding and interpreting these cultural characteristics. The method of the book is to discuss everyday phenomena and trace the underlying cultural factors.

The book offers a glimpse into the meaning of Chinese culture, but suggests a possible method for a deeper understanding of Chinese life.

Cathy Xiaoxia Zhou

Contents

GREETINGS AND INTRODUCTIONS

Have You eaten?

Chīguo fàn le?

Chīguo le.

Yes.

Have you eaten?

"Have you eaten?" is simply a common greeting in China, not a invitation to dinner.

Don't expect this is an invitation to have a meal together if your Chinese friend asks you this question. The expression is used simply as a common greeting in China. Since it is only a greeting instead of a genuine question, you can usually give a positive answer like " Yes, I've eaten. Have you?".

This special greeting can be interpreted in two ways: the Chinese care about eating or it indicates that there was not enough food to eat in the past. Just as Americans like to greet people " How are you doing?"or British " Nice day, isn't it?" to show their first concern, this Chinese greeting also reflects the priority of the Chinese people.

Nowadays, as China has adapted to a market economy and eating is no longer the top concern, the popular greeting has changed to " Are you busy?(忙吗? Máng ma?)". The change indicates the shifted priority from food to occupation.The positive answer to this question conveys that you are still working, while the negative answer

3

Zuìjìn máng ma?

Tǐng máng de.

Yes. Quite busy.

Are you busy recently?

"Are you busy? *(Máng ma?)*" is a popular greeting in today's Chinese society, especially in the urban areas.

suggests probably you will be laid off or have been laid off. Another common greeting in China is " Where are you going?(去哪儿啊?Qù nǎr a?)". Since it is not a request

Nín qù nǎr a?

O, zǒuzou.

Oh, just have a walk.

Where are you going?

5

for information, a vague answer like " Just have a walk" will do.

Sometimes you will find your Chinese friend greeting you like "You are reading?" when he/she sees you hav-

Shìde.

Yes.

Zài děng chē a ?

Waiting for the bus?

It's common that the Chinese greet their friends by stating what they're doing at the time.

6

ing a book in hand. It is very common that the Chinese greet their friends by stating something obvious as "You are doing your washing?", or "You are waiting for the bus?" etc. The answer to such greetings can be a smile or just a "yes".

The most misleading greeting is that your neighbor or the guard downstairs will greet you as "You're back?(Huílái le?)" or "You're going out?(Chūqu a?)" when he/she sees you coming in or going out of the building. Don't think he/she is spying on you. Rather it is just a simple way of making contact. The response to that is also a smile and a "yes".

☺ *On most occasions, the above-mentioned are the common greeting methods among Chinese themselves. The most frequently used word for them to greet a foreign friend is still* "Nǐ hǎo" *(Hello).*

Hello and Happiness

姚 明

Yáo Míng

☺ *Chinese names are always a good topic to start a conversation. NBA player Yao Ming's self-introduction serves as a good example.*

My first name, Ming, means "light". To write it, you use two Chinese characters. The first character means "the sun," and the second one means "the moon." The two names together mean light all the time, day and night.

My last name Yao doesn't mean anything in itself. It is just a last name like Jones. But the two characters that are used to write it, when looked at separately do mean something. The first character means woman. The second character means many, many, many , like a billion, only more. So that means more than Wilt Chamberlain, right?...

From *A Life in Two Worlds*

When you overhear the above greeting, don't feel surprised. "Happiness"(喜 xǐ or 欢 huān in Mandarin) is a common Chinese given name for a male or female. Unlike the given names used in Christian countries, which are mostly from the Bible like "Adam, Joseph, Mary and Sarah, etc", the Chinese given names indicate a variety of meanings. Some indicate the good wishes and high expectation of the new parents to their babies while some others convey the love of nature and the actual facts concerning the birth. The common given names with auspicious meanings are 运 yùn (fortune), 欢 huān/喜 xǐ (happiness), 贵 guì (preciousness), 毅 yì(tenacity), 忠 zhōng (loyalty), 信 xìn(trust), 聪 cōng (cleverness),丽 lì (beauty), 智 zhì(wisdom), 伟 wěi (greatness), 瑞 ruì(good sign), 祥 xiáng(good omen).

Those common names indicating love of nature and the facts of birth can be found in names like: 川 chuān (river), 峰 fēng(mountain top), 花 huā (flower), 玉 yù

10

(jade),晓霞 xiǎo xiá(morning sunshine),燕 yàn (swallow) indicating spring;菊 jú(chrysanthemum) indicating autumn; 梅 méi(plum) indicating winter or 京生 jīng shēng(born in Beijing); 思杭 sī háng (missing Hangzhou) indicating the family origin etc.

While the fact that the Chinese names have specific meanings is one noticeable feature, another noticeable feature, which differs from most countries, is that the Chinese given names always follow their family names. And women don't use their husbands' family names after marriage in Mainland China. There are more than two thousand family names. The most common ones are 李 lǐ, 张 zhāng, and 王 wáng.

The Chinese names contain spectra of cultural information, which can serve as an appropriate topic to start a conversation, and actually it is one of the favorite topics the Chinese enjoy talking about. The process of exploring the meaning will probably lead you to a close friendship.

> * What's your name?
>   **Nǐ jiào shénme míngzi ?**
>   你叫什么名字?
> * My name is...
>   **Wǒ jiào ...**
>   我叫······
> * What's your family name?
>   **Nǐ xìng shénme ?**
>   你姓什么?
> * My family name is...
>   **Wǒ xìng...**
>   我姓······

Using "Ni Hao"

"Nǐ Hǎo", functioning as "Hello" or "Hi" in English, is the most common greeting in China. The expression can be used at any time and on any occasion. However, it is not frequently used among the Chinese themselves. The Chinese employ different greetings upon different persons. For example, they will use "Nín Hǎo" to address somebody senior in age or position instead of "Nǐ Hǎo" to show respect. And they will greet people with their titles, such as "Jīnglǐ Hǎo"(Hello, Manager) or "Zhǔrèn Hǎo" (Hello, Director). Possibly if they notice that you have a sore throat, they would add some words after the greeting to show their concerns, such as "Have you got a cold?(你感冒了吗?Nǐ gǎnmào le ma?)", "Have you put on enough clothes?(你衣服穿够了吗?Nǐ yīfu chuān gòu le ma?)" or "You should drink more hot water.(你要多喝点开水。Nǐ yào duō hē diǎn kāishuǐ.)", which would sound sometimes annoying to your ears as if the person intrudes too much into your privacy.

13

Shaking Hands

Hands shaking, as a courtesy, was introduced to China just decades ago. It is still not quite commonly practised in the rural areas of China. Even if it is popular in the urban regions, you will find hands shaking in China is not naturally adopted. Most Chinese still don't know when to offer their hands, how to hold the offered hand, and for how long to hold the offered hand. You will often find only your fingers are lightly held or touched

to be exact. Or sometimes you will find the Chinese
will not offer their hands at all when they are introduced.
Instead, most likely they will make a nodding or slight
bowing. Of course, they won't bow to their waists as
the Japanese do.

Traditional Chinese courtesies equivalent to hands
shaking are kneeling (The Chinese use "kowtow") and
cupping one's hands before one's chest. In the past,
children used to kneel before their parents every morning
to pay their respects, and the magistrates to the emperor.
Nowadays, when people express their deep respect or
gratitude, they will still kneel. As for cupping hands
before the chest, people sometimes use this gesture and
at the same time with the expression "Glad to meet you.
(幸会幸会。Xìnghuì xìnghuì.)". Cupping hands is
also often used when you greet people on New Year's
Day with an accompanying expression "Wishing you
good fortune.(万事如意！Wànshì rúyì!)".

Nowadays cupping hands is only commonly used during New Year's Day.

"What's Your Sign?"

 Rat 鼠 shǔ

 Ox 牛 niú

 Tiger 虎 hǔ

 Rabbit 兔 tù

 Dragon 龙 lóng

 Snake 蛇 shé

 Horse 马 mǎ

 Sheep 羊 yáng

 Monkey 猴 hóu

 Rooster 鸡 jī

 Dog 狗 gǒu

 Pig 猪 zhū

When a Chinese person tells you that he/she is a dragon, he/she is telling you his/her age. In China, apart from employing the solar system, they also keep their own lunar system. As China used to be an agrarian economy, which depended heavily on the cycle of the seasons and climate, astrology was well developed. Their lunar calendar, created almost 5,000 years ago, was based on a 60-year cycle of the combination of the 10 "Heavenly Stems" and 12 "Earthly Branches". The 12 Earthly Branches were governed by the twelve–year lunar cycle. Later the 12 Earthly Branches were given signs named after animals – rat, ox, tiger, rabbit, dragon, snake, horse, sheep, monkey, rooster, dog and pig. These 12 Earthly Branches have their counterpart in the West in the solar signs. They are Rat to Sagittarius; Ox to Capricorn; Tiger to Aquarius; Rabbit to Pisces; Dragon to Aries; Snake to Taurus; Horse to Gemini; Sheep to Cancer; Monkey to Leo; Rooster to Virgo; Dog to Libra and Pig to Scorpio.

Nowadays the Chinese don't usually ask people their age directly as they did before, but they still know that by using indirect way such as asking the animal sign he/she is. The recent 12 cycle goes like this: Rat 1996, Ox 1997, Tiger 1998, Rabbit 1999, Dragon 2000, Snake 2001, Horse 2002, Sheep 2003, Monkey 2004, Rooster 2005, Dog 2006, Pig 2007.

The animal signs, with each animal's basic character type, also indicate the personality of the person born in the specific animal year, the core of the Chinese horoscopes. Discussion of the animal signs is also a favorite topic to start a conversion with the Chinese.

M: *I'm a sheep. What about you?*
   Wǒ shǔ yáng. Nǐ ne ?

F: *(Cool) I'm a tiger.*
   Wǒ shǔ hǔ.

Discussion of animal signs is a favorite topic among the Chinese.

GETTING ALONG WITH CHINESE ETIQUETTE

In the Home

Normally the Chinese will invite the guests to dinner at home by word of mouth. Unlike westerners who will likely make the invitation a week or days ahead, the Chinese will probably make the invitation just one day or even hours ahead, which sometimes causes inconvenience.

When you are invited to a Chinese home, remember to bring a gift with you as a token for respect. This is part of the Chinese courtesy. The common thing to bring is fruit or some ready-made food. Of course a bottle of wine or some chocolate are also popular nowadays. As for the time to arrive, the Chinese are not particular about that. Probably the Chinese food is cooked and served after guests are present, not like Western cooking, which is baked or roasted to make it ready just for the time when the guests arrive. Generally speaking, the Chinese will arrive earlier either to give a helping hand to the hostess or to have a casual chat with the hostess before the other guests arrive. Of course, five to ten minutes late won't cause any noticeable inconvenience.

It is not common for the host and hostess to meet you at the door to take your coat. Remember to observe the household custom to change into slippers upon entering. After you are seated, you will most likely be offered the Chinese green tea. It is not the Chinese custom to ask your preference for drinks.

For family gatherings, the Chinese don't observe very rigid formality. For example, you will not be introduced to the other guests. So you should take the initiative to make yourself known and welcomed by the others.

While at the table, the seat facing the east or the south is reserved for the honored guest. As for the round table, the guest of honor sits directly across from the host, who takes the least honorable seat near the serving door. The host will usually apologize in advance, according to the Chinese courtesy, for the meager and ill-prepared meal about to be served. But what waits for you are like a banquet with eight or ten cold dishes first and then an-

The host will usually apologize in advance, according to the Chinese courtesy, for the meager and ill-prepared meal about to be served.

other eight or ten hot dishes. The dishes, not served course by course as you do in your country, are all presented at the table (If you eat in a restaurant, the course is served one by one by a waiter or waitress). And everybody shares them from the common plates (Part of the Chinese mentality, everybody shares equally everything).

The host or the hostess will keep putting food to your plate as soon as you have finished yours. To the Chinese, to leave the guest not fully filled is impolite, while to a westerner not finishing the food on his/her own plate is impolite. The very misunderstanding conception will always cause you to overeat. So to save yourself from overeating, leave food on your plate when you cannot eat any more. Under no circumstances should you put the food back. It is the Chinese courtesy for the host to prepare more than enough for the guests. If everything is finished on the table, it will embarrass the host and hostess because it means they don't treat the guests well and they are not generous enough.

As the meal is the most important for the gathering, guests will leave soon after the meal to allow time for the hostess to do the cleaning. A polite way for you to excuse yourself is to say, "You must be tired. I'll let you have a good rest."

Table Manners

Sit down after the guest of honor is seated. The meal usually begins with a toast by the host. Stand up when the host is making a toast. During the mealtime, the guests are also supposed to propose toasts in turn in honor of the host and the other guests.

The most challenging thing for a foreign guest at the Chinese table is to hold the chopsticks properly. Always grab the chopsticks in the middle, making sure that the ends are even. Do not wave chopsticks above dishes. Do not stick chopsticks vertically into a bowl of rice. If you cannot do with them, it is proper to ask for a spoon.

In most part of China, when chopsticks are put vertically into a bowl of rice, it indicates the food is for the dead.

Put your chopsticks on the chopstick support when you're not using them. (If the support isn't prepared, put them horizontally on a plate.)

27

Don't expect the meat will be served after the bones are removed. Meat with bones is thought tastier, and thus more expensive. So you will find the Chinese eating chicken claws and wings instead of the chicken fillet. For foods containing bones (such as chicken), hold the food with the chopsticks and eat around the bone. Do not use your fingers.

Fish is usually served whole on the table. Do not turn it over if there is a sailor or anyone at the table who has a friend or relative as a sailor.

Throughout the meal, the guests are supposed to pay elaborate compliments to the food and the cooking skills of the hostess.

When you are offered tea or wine, bend your index finger and middle finger to tap on the table three or four times to express your appreciation.

Guests are supposed to pay elaborate compliments
to the food.

In a Restaurant

The Chinese love to eat out, especially when they entertain guests. This habit results in the abundance of restaurants everywhere. Eating together, like the westerners drinking in pubs or bars with friends, is a social gathering, a thanksgiving for the food, a celebration of family ties and the bonds of friendship.

Unlike in a western restaurant that every diner will be offered a menu, in a Chinese restaurant, one menu is offered to the entire table even if there are a dozen of diners. Normally the one who receives the menu and orders the food will pay for the table. Or the one who sits near the door will pay for the table. The Chinese find " splitting the bill" very ungracious and embarrassing. The common practice is that the other diners will take turns to pay for the meals later. The courses ordered will be cold dishes and hot ones. Normally the last course served is soup. Fruit served at last will be regarded as dessert.

Unlike the courtesies of some cultures that require people to eat quietly, the Chinese like to talk loudly when eating in restaurants. Most likely, the guests will challenge each other to drinking games throughout the meal.

At the meal table, the diners usually let their formal hair down, expose their personal preferences and try to demonstrate their goodwill and friendship by sharing the food together. So some people take advantage of this opportunity to have their business done at the table. Some use food and drink as one of their primary tools in creating and sustaining cooperative relationship with other people.

☺ *You may have your business done at the table.*

Eating is Heaven

shí

The frequently heard expression " Eating is heaven," reflects how food-conscious the Chinese are. In fact, when you wander around any city in China, the most obvious you find is the abundance of restaurants. Although a great Chinese sage mentioned some two thousand years ago that food and sex are the natural desires of human beings, with sex being suppressed due to the rigid moral codes, food has become the strongest obsession.

The Chinese cuisine, which has been developed for thousands of years, is more than just basic nourishment. It must be a feast for the eyes, please the palate by its flavor and taste and ensure optimum health. To be a feast for the eyes means that every dish presented is not only to satisfy one's stomach, but also to appeal to one's eyes. As a Chinese idiom goes "the beauty and elegance can serve as food(秀色可餐 xiùsè kě cān) ", to make the food beautiful is the first priority. Food preparation and presentation with colors are the most creative process. And to enhance the beauty of each dish, the Chinese will use containers different in shapes and materials to present the food. How to please the palate is of great importance. The Chinese food enjoys its reputation for its different flavoring. There are sauces of every flavor, including ingredients with strong aromas such as scallions, ginger, garlic, chili peppers, wine, star anise, sesame oil, and so on. The food served is always made blending with the flavors of the ingredients. To ensure the taste, freshness is the preferred state of all the Chinese ingredients. No wonder when you order fish, seafood or whatever can be prepared alive in a restaurant, the chef will show you what you have ordered is fresh before he cooks. Besides freshness, the Chinese have created various methods to cook different foods, which are manifested from the rich verbs about cooking in the Chinese language. The most common verbs include 炒 chǎo (stir frying), 炸 zhá (deep frying), 煮 zhǔ (boiling) and 炖 dùn (stewing), etc.

Cooking and eating are so important that the Chinese use them as metaphors to describe abstract ideas. For example, Mencius once compared the skills to run a country to baking a small fish (Both need precaution and patience). Another example is that the Chinese classify people either as "cooked" or "raw". For the "cooked" they will treat them as friends, while the "raw" are treated as strangers.

The Chinese believe in the medicinal value of food. They prepare and eat food according to their ancient Yin-yang principle, which holds that everything in the universe is either Yin (negative, cold or wet) or Yang (positive, hot or dry), and the food that one eats must be a harmonious balance of these cosmic forces if one is to stay physically, emotionally and spiritually healthy. For example, beef and chicken are thought not suitable to eat in summer because they belong to the category of hot food. Instead, watermelon and green beans are thought to be ideal for summer.

The Chinese chefs take Yin-yang theory to their cooking as well. Generally speaking, Yin would be the milder flavors while Yang would be the bolder flavors. What the chefs strive for is the balance of the taste. For example, sweet and sour, hot and sour, and strong flavored dishes paired with plain rice are all examples of Yin-yang balanced foods. When preparing these dishes the chef is always careful to balance the opposing flavors. Sweet and Sour Shrimp that is all sweet or overly sour wouldn't be very pleasing to the palate and wouldn't be good. And pairing a spicy dish with other spicy dishes would overtax the taste buds. Yin and Yang can also be used to explain the appeal of dishes featuring a mixture of soft or delicate foods with crunchy or crisp foods. Tofu dishes with chopped nuts or diced water chestnuts always balance these textural differences. A plate full of crunchy food could tire the mouth, while a plate full of soft food might not seem very fulfilling.

☺ *The famous Chinese saying:* 民 *mín(people)* 以 *yǐ(consider)* 食 *shí (food)* 为 *wéi(to be)* 天 *tiān (heaven).* —— *Eating is heaven.*

Well, he is from Sichuan, while she is from Shanghai.

☺ In China, people from east China, such as Zhejiang Province and Shanghai, are known to favorite sweet flavor, while people from west China, especially Sichuan Province, are known to enjoy spicy-hot flavor.

Nodding Doesn't Always Mean "Yes"

While you are talking to a Chinese person, you will find him/her keeping nodding to what you have said. The gesture will incur the misunderstanding because nodding usually conveys the message of approval to what the speaker has said to most peoples of the world. However, in China it doesn't always carry the same meaning as most peoples assume. On most occasions, nodding simply suggests that the listener is listening. Why? Because in China people (except close friends or lovers) seldom have eye contacts when they are talking to each other. If you stare at the speaker in a conversation, you will be regarded either to challenge his/her authority or have some evil intention, thus disrespectful. Therefore, to keep the conversation going, nodding serves as an indicator that " I'm listening".

The Color Red

If you do not know what to wear to attend a Chinese celebration, something red is always the right choice on such occasions. The red color is always associated with "happiness and good fortune". It is symbolic of fire and wards off evil spirits. The Chinese people enjoy decorating their houses with something red (e.g. red couplets on both sides of the gate; red paper-cuts on the window; red character " 福 fú" on the door etc) during the Spring Festival (the biggest holiday in China) and wedding celebrations. The bride wears a traditional Chinese wedding dress in red on her wedding day (though probably influenced by the western customs she would wear white wedding dress at the beginning of the celebration). Unlike the connotation of red to "anger, danger and the irrational outburst of emotions" in the West, such as the expressions like: be a red rag to a bull; to see red; to see the red light; to paint the town red; red in tooth and claw etc, the red always carries commendatory implications in China. Red loving customs can be traced back to the ancient worship of the fire, which always shelters people with warmth and safety.

The next color used to be very special is yellow, which resembles the color of earth and soil. Since China used to be an agrarian society, earth and soil were very important to them. Yellow used to be the exclusive color used by the Emperors in China.

Another favorite color is green, which represents life and vitality, while black and white are associated with death. Don't wear a black dress to attend the wedding or a birthday party. Wearing white headdress indicates that someone in your home recently dies.

Probably black is also associated with darkness. The Chinese like to refer to things illegally done "black", for example, "black money" and "black market". And "black heart" refers to someone really bad.

The implied meanings of colors are conspicuous in the costumes of traditional Chinese operas. Red indicates loyalty and courage; black represents integrity and impartiality; yellow apparel signifies royalty and white to purity.

Don't wear a green hat on any occasion in your daily life. "Wearing a green hat" is a Chinese idiom referring to one's wife has committed an adultery. A husband wearing a green hat seems to claim that his wife is an adulteress. Therefore don't make yourself a standing joke.

The Great Harmonious World

With their interaction with the nature, the early Chinese developed their unique understanding of the relations between man and the physical cosmos, on which this philosophic influence is still exerted. They believed that man was only one component, not different from any other animate forms in the universe. The ultimate efforts of humans were to maintain and sustain the harmonious relationships with all the elements of the universe. These efforts can be illustrated in the Chinese myths and legends, e.g. "Da Yu Curbs the Flood"（大禹治水 **Dà Yǔ zhìshuǐ**）, which gives an account how Da Yu dug canals and built banks to facilitate the water flow before it formed flood.

This principle, when applied to the human relations, is tinged with special Chinese morality, which is well illustrated in the Confucian classic work 《《中庸》》 **zhōngyōng** (*The Mean*). The Chinese tend to seek the common grounds between each other while avoiding direct confrontation. They prefer facilitating the win-win approach instead of competition. In another word, they always follow what they think the Way to Heaven, mutual or multi-lateral benefits. They will try to seek the optimum ways to get desired results, defuse antagonism and find the most workable approach among their partners. There is an abundance of Chinese idioms reflecting this philosophic thinking, like "to live harmoniously between each other"; "Harmony is what matters" and "Harmony will lead to wealth and fortune", etc.

The physical evidence of this abstract philosophic approach can be seen by the shape of 圆 (round circle). Visitors will find the Chinese cherish round things, such as the full moon, the round lanterns and the round table, etc. To the Chinese, the round means perfection with no pointed angles. No wonder the Temple of Heaven (highly sacred ground of course for emperors to perform the major ceremonial rites) was built in the round shape.

The Chinese would also be criticised by their inclination to seek harmony as no principle by peoples of different cultures. Avoiding confrontation and conflicts sometimes lead the Chinese to tell white lies in efforts not to tell unpleasant truths.

One Promise is Worth a Thousand Bars of Gold

Whereas the West and other cultures depend on the laws and contracts guiding their public and business life, the traditional Chinese rely on their sincerity in their interaction with other people either in private or business situations, thus interpersonal relationship based on trust

46

is well developed in China. As the saying goes "exchanging hearts between each other", the Chinese will sincerely expose themselves to those whom they trust in personality. So a promise by mouth is kept as seriously as the written contract.

The reason that the Chinese have well developed interpersonal relations can be explained from traditional lifestyle. China used to be an agrarian society, and the majority of its people were farmers, who lived a settled life. This static situation helped to develop close personal relationships, especially among the family clan or those living in the same village. So it is natural that they prefer to trust those they know rather than the intangible rigid rules and laws.

Their preference to put trust in individuals rather than in institutions and laws will make it difficult for foreigners to do business with them and for them to deal effectively with foreign corporations.

Social Distance

The distance you keep when you talk to others reveals your culture. Generally speaking, westerners like to keep 2-4 feet as the personal zone when they talk in earnest about something. Asians are accustomed to talking to others from a closer distance. The Chinese like to be within arms' reach or closer when they are talking. Unlike western practice, it is very common to see two persons of the same gender walking and talking together with one's arm on another's shoulder, or two women talking hand in hand. Generally speaking, the persons of the same gender keep a closer distance in the public than those of different gender. It is against traditional Chinese values to show love and affection in public. So there was no hugging no kissing, even no hand-shaking in public in old days.

Contrary to what one might think, the distance the Chinese keep to strangers is less than that to their ordinary friends. In an experiment, a sociologist randomly chose twenty persons and asked them to get on board a small van. They did squeeze in with no distance in between at the beginning. Then they were arranged to know each other and became friends. A few

days later, they were asked to get on board the same van, but they failed in getting all in.

The experiment shows that the Chinese treat their friends differently from strangers. Among friends, they have certain respect, which prevent them to elbow against each other. In another word, the Chinese behave more decently in the presence of ones they know. So you will find a well-behaved child in the presence of parents; good pupils before teachers, and so on. As to strangers, they are not that alert of their behaviours and the incurring consequences. The ill behaviours, such as elbowing one's way through the crowd, jaywalking across the street and jumping the queue, are not hard to understand.

Interesting Numbers

Wang's telephone number is 68888...and he lives in Room 888, 8th floor, 888 xxx Road.

8 (bā) with its homonym to "fortune" (fā), is the most favored number in China.

Numbers to the Chinese are of vital importance. The Chinese always extend associative meanings to them. Even numbers, having the associative meaning of doubleness, are specially favored by the Chinese. You will find when the Chinese order dishes in restaurant, most likely the courses will be even-numbered as four, six, eight, ten or twelve. When a guest comes for visit with fruit, the number will be even-numbered as well. So do the gifts to the newly-weds. When the Chinese buy flats, the even-numbered floors are always the first to be sold out. "Eight" with its homonym to "fortune" is the most favored number, while "four" with its homonym to "death" is least popular among all the even numbers.

Some odd-numbers are also favored. The number five is especially significant because it relates to the cornerstone of Chinese culture: the five elements (metal, wood, water, fire and earth) of nature. The Chinese classify five tastes (sweet, sour, salty, bitter and pungent) and five basic col-

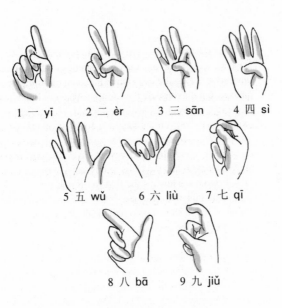

Common Chinese Gestures for Numbers

ors (red, green, yellow, back and white). The ideal family is having the five-generation under the same roof and the ideal family size is five (three boys and two girls). The number one, as a Chinese idiom goes "one heart and one soul (meaning with undivided attention)", is favored by young lovers. A boy is likely to send one flower to his lover to express his undivided love. Or he will choose to send nine flowers, for nine (*jiǔ*), a homonym of the word "forever (*jiǔ*)", indicates his love will last forever. Of course, influenced by western culture, thirteen is not welcomed by the Chinese as well.

Giving Gifts

Never give the clock as a present because sending the clock (pronounced as "sòng zhōng") is the homonym to "attending a funeral".

As we keep saying that interpersonal relationship is very developed in China, one manifestation is the common practice of gift giving. Giving gifts is a required courtesy. For example, when you go to visit someone for the first time; when you come back from a trip; when you go visiting someone's home; when you visit the sick in a hospital; when you go to see your teacher, you are supposed to take a gift with you. The gift you send is a token to show your consideration and respect. Generally speaking, do not send an expensive gift to an ordinary friend or someone you pay the first visit. If you do, the person receiving the gift will think you bribe him/her, or you want a favour from him/her. Of course, there are people who take advantage of this age-old practice for their personal ends.

The common gifts people give are sweets, fruits, chocolates, tea, wine or some local specialities you have bought from your trip.

Some taboos concerning gift giving: don't send apples and pears to the sick in the hospital because "apple" is the homonym to "death" and "pear" to "separating". Neither does sending chrysanthemums because this flower is for funeral.

Also if you attend a wedding ceremony, never give the clock as a present because sending the clock (pronounced as "sòng zhōng") is the homonym to "attending a funeral". Instead give peanuts, dates, longan and lotus seeds, which indicate longevity and many children, etc.

Remember when you give or receive presents (including business cards), use both hands to show your sincerity and respect. Using both hands originally indicates that you do not bear arms when you approach the other party. This age-old courtesy is still kept in our daily practice.

Understanding Chinese Girls

Unlike Western girls who dream about having healthy and tanned skins, the Chinese girls like to keep their skin pale. So you will notice that there is array of whitening cosmetics products in the Chinese department stores, and umbrellas are absolute daily necessity for girls in the summer to prevent from getting suntanned. Having suntanned skin indicates either rustic farmers or manual laborers, thus lacking elegance and sophistication.

Influenced consciously or unconsciously by the traditional values, Chinese girls are desired to be docile and family-oriented. Too much exposure of personal emotions is against the traditions. Most likely you will find the Chinese girls put their hands in front of their mouths to hide their teeth when they smile. They will turn bashful and bend their heads down when required to answer questions. They seldom have eye contact when talking to males.

Saving Face

The Chinese are renowned for their hospitality. They will shower visitors and guests with volume of food and drink that cost far more than they can afford and that is more than their guests can possibly consume.

The Chinese seldom say "no" to anyone who is asking for help. To avoid any response that is negative and might be upsetting, they will choose to speak in vague. So do not insist on, otherwise you will breach the etiquette, thus making the one lose face.

Where? Where?

Modesty is one of the traditional virtues the great sage Confucius (551-479B.C) advocated. Although a great scholar, Confucius admonished his students, "When walking in the company of three, there must be one I can learn from"(三人行，必有我师焉。Sān rén xíng, bì yǒu wǒ shī yān.). To Confucius modesty and humility are required qualities for a society to sustain itself while pride will lead to destruction.

The typical example of the modesty is demonstrated by the host to his visitors. He will apologize the ill-preparation and small quantity of his food, which turns out to be sumptuous banquet. And the modesty is also shown when the Chinese accept compliments. They always respond to compliments with "Nǎli nǎli. (literally where?

Where?)"—figuratively meaning, "I have done nothing to deserve your compliment."

Another common way to show the Chinese modesty is that the Chinese often politely refuse offers of drinks, refreshments, gifts and other favors two or three times before graciously accepting them. Their modesty requires them not to open the gifts before the sender.

Their modesty requires them not to challenge but to respect, which results in a low profile of Chinese. This is sometimes misunderstood as no ambition or competitive spirit. Their modesty leads them more to group-consciousness rather than to individual-consciousness.

CHINESE TRADITIONS
AND CULTURE

Holiday Celebrations

Holiday observations betray more than anything else to reflect one civilization. With their own unique development, the Chinese have developed their own holidays and celebrations, which are less religious than their Western counterparts.

There are three most important holidays, i.e. the Spring Festival, the Dragon Boat Festival and the Mid-Autumn Festival.

Spring Festival

(春节 Chūnjié)

The biggest holiday observed is the Spring Festival, which falls on the first day of the first new moon after the sun enters Aquarius (around the middle of January to later February of the Western calendar). Traditionally, the festival begins with making a special porridge with eight ingredients of grains or rice topped with nuts and dried fruits on the 8th of the last lunar month and lasts until the 15th of the first lunar month called Lantern Festival. During the month-long celebration, the Chinese will engage in making offering of sweets to the Kitchen God on the 23rd of the last lunar moon. They will also be busy cleaning and decorating the house with auspicious signs and talismans of good luck and good fortune, which the Chinese believe will ward off evil and attract good luck for the New Year. The most important thing for a family is, of course, busy preparing the New Year food.

The climax of the month-long celebration falls on the New Year's Eve, for every member of the family returns home to share a sumptuous dinner together. Fish, as one indispensable course, will be served whole and can only be eaten half and the rest will be saved for the new year (The Chinese word for "Fish" 鱼 yú rhymes with the word "surplus" 余 yú). Children will receive "red envelopes" containing gifts of lucky money called (yāsuìqián) which are put under their pillows that night to keep them safe for the coming new year.

Before eating the sumptuous dinner, firecrackers will be given off. And at midnight, the New Year is ushered in with another exploding firecrackers. On New Year's Day the first thing to do is to give off firecrackers again to welcome the coming of the New Year. To the Chinese the firecrackers will ward off the evil spirit and venerate the gods.

The New Year's breakfast usually includes some special foods: one of them is 糕 gāo (a kind of cake made of ground glutinous rice which is essential to be eaten on the New Year's day, for GAO rhymes with the word "high" 高 gāo to mean a step higher in the coming new year). In some families, noodles will be eaten to mean longevity. And another common food is jiǎozi (a kind of dumpling with fillings inside) to mean having a son in the coming year.

A round of visits to relatives and friends will follow after breakfast. Nowadays, with the popularity of telephones, people usually make calls to express their wishes to their beloved ones. All the telephone lines and cables will be engaged on this day.

In the towns and villages, roving bands of musicians (e.g. the dragon dance) parade through the streets stopping at every door to announce the arrival of spring. Each family presents the groups with "red envelopes" with money inside. Children, in new clothes, collect more "red envelopes" from their relatives they visit.

Since this is also a holiday for family reunion and visits of relatives, the whole country is on a run. It is hard to get tickets to travel around.

☺ *Useful vocabulary for the holiday:*

春联 chūnlián
Spring Festival couplets

鞭炮 biānpào
Firecrackers

饺子 **jiǎozi**
Jiaozi

压岁钱 **yāsuìqián**
Lucky money for Spring Festival

Dragon Boat Festival

(端午节 Duānwǔ jié)

The Dragon Boat Festival falls on the fifth day of the fifth moon of the lunar calendar.

As for its origin, there are different versions. One of the popular versions goes back to the period of Warring States (403BC-221 BC) concerning a famous Chinese scholar-statesman named Qu Yuan, who served the King of Chu. As a loyal minister, Qu offered counsels in favour of his country. But through the intrigues of his rivals, he was discredited and found himself in disfavour. On the fifth day of the fifth moon in the year 295 BC, Qu, in despair, drowned himself in the Miluo River in Hunan Province. Loving his uprightness and honesty, the people living around the river rushed out in their boats in an attempt to search for him.

The unsuccessful rescue attempt later has become one part of the festivities for this festival—Dragon Boat Racing Competition. On the occasion, each plain boat will be decorated with the head and tail of a dragon, a mythological creature regarded by the Chinese as having dominion of the waters and exerting control over rainfall. The decoration process culminating in the dotting of the eyes of the dragon with the paint used to be a solemn religious ceremony presided over by a Taoist priest. During the competition, each boat has one drum player who controls the pace of the rowing and the rowers must have the same speed to ensure the straightness of the boat. People standing on both sides of the river cheer for their team, a spectacular view of the spring.

Another tradition for this festival is to hang calamus and artemisia (both are plants with aromatic flavour used as herbal medicine) above their doors as a preventive against pestilence, which occurs frequently during this time of the year because of the warm weather and the humidity. And people eat food and drink wine with realgar inside, which they think will prevent diseases and promote a healthy digestive system. People also use realgar or cinnabar to paint their children's foreheads with the ideograph 王, and fasten amulets containing spices or medicines (called fragrance bag) to their clothes in some parts of China. The fragrance bags are exquisite in embroidery and highly valued among some people in rural areas.

The typical food for this festival is "zong zi" with glutinous rice wrapped in bamboo leaves.

粽子 zòngzi

Mid-Autumn Festival

(中秋节 Zhōngqiū jié)

As its name portrays, this festival is celebrated on the fifteenth day of the eighth moon (the autumn) of the lunar calendar. As one of the three most important traditional festivals, Mid-Autumn Festival is most romanticised in China as a day of family reunion and a festival with friends. On the night of the day (as the saying goes this day enjoys the fullest moon with the most brilliance), the family or friends sit together enjoying the beautiful food on the table with the bright moon in the sky.

The indispensable food for this festival is the moon cakes. There are varieties of moon cakes (baked pastry) with different ingredients: lotus seed paste, bean paste, mixed nuts, dried fruits, ham and salted egg yolk, etc. Nowadays there are even ice-cream moon cakes as well.

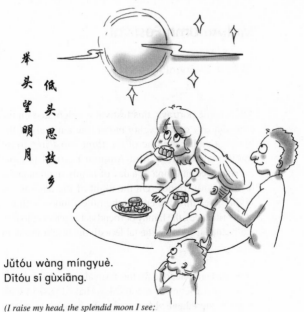

Jǔtóu wàng míngyuè.
Dītóu sī gùxiāng.

*(I raise my head, the splendid moon I see;
Then droop my head, and sink to dreams of my hometown.)*

Lantern Festival

(元宵节 Yuánxiāo jié)

The Lantern Festival, on the fifteenth day after New Year, marks the end of the New Year festivities. This holiday evolved from ancient Chinese beliefs that celestial spirits could be seen flying about in the light of the first full moon of the lunar calendar. This tradition is still seen by displays of colorful lanterns on the buildings, trees and streets.

People also dub this holiday as the Chinese Carnival, for there used to be parades with people dancing in different shapes of lanterns as dragons, lions and lotuses etc. as well as walking on stilts. These activities were used to be participated by the whole village. And the villages competed with each other to gain the award of the best display of lights and dances in the parade.

The day is also called the Chinese Valentine's day because young ladies were allowed to go out to see the lanterns and other festivities on the streets (to see the celestial spirits, so to say) that night, which would provide chances for young men and women to find ones they love (In old days, young girls were not allowed to go out of their living quarters).

Like the most Chinese festivals, this holiday has its own special food called "yuan xiao". These dumplings, which are made of rice flour, are round, symbolizing both the first full moon of the lunar New Year and the complete family reunion so cherished by the traditional Chinese.

元宵 yuánxiāo

Qing Ming (Tomb-Sweeping Day)

(清明节 Qīngmíng jié)

Qing Ming, roughly on April 4th or 5th in the solar calendar each year, is a special day to pay tribute to ancestors' resting places in China, equivalent to the All Saints' Day in the West. On this day families will sweep and manicure the tombs of their ancestors and place fresh flowers. Offerings of meats, vegetables, and wine are placed in front of the tombs. Other offerings, like paper money and other symbols of wealth specially printed for this purpose, are burned in the belief that they will be transformed into the real wealth for their ancestors to use in the other world.

The origin of Qing Ming can be traced back to the early Chinese civilization, which shows how the ancient Chinese feel for the land from which they sprang. Visits to the tombs of ancestors remind the descendants of the family origin and the inseparable tie with the land they belong to. An illustration to show how the Chinese fervently respect this bond is evidenced by the custom of carrying a small amount of actual soil from their home as an amulet when travelling afar. A well-known Chinese idiom further illustrates the bond, i.e. "Tree leaves will eventually return to their root"(叶落归根 yè luò guī gēn).

Traditionally, tombs are on the hillsides. To climb hills in early spring help resume strength after a long winter to get ready for a busy new season.

So on this day people will go to the tombs with solemnness and return with light heart, and perhaps carry in hands some wild flowers collected from the mountains and hills.

The Seventh Eve

(七夕 Qīxī)

This traditional holiday falls on the 7th of the seventh month. It originates from a beautiful legend of the stellar lovers Weaver Maid and Draught Ox. They were cruelly separated from each other by the sky river by the father of Weaver Maid, who thought Weaver Maid neglected her weaving by indulgence in love. They were, however, allowed to meet each other only on the seventh of the seventh month. It is said all the birds, especially the magpies will form a bridge for the poor couple to get across.

This love story, though sad, has been loved by women. They place fruits under the moonlight that day and pray for abundant descendants and the weaving skills. Therefore, it is also called the Daughter's Day or the Chinese Valentine's Day.

The Double Ninth Holiday

(重阳节 Chóngyáng jié)

The Chongyang Festival (also known as the Double Ninth Festival) falls on the ninth day of the ninth month of the Chinese lunar calendar.

Traditionally, as the last outing of the year before the onset of winter, this day is specially set aside for families to go hiking, flying kites and climbing mountains. People also carry a special plant called dogwood (a plant with strong fragrance), which will protect them from getting ill. And people will drink chrysanthemum wine while appreciating the beauty of the chrysanthemums. So this day is also called Height-climbing Day or Chrysanthemum Day. The special food for this day is Chongyang Cake (a homonym of the Chinese word for "high").

This holiday is observed as the Seniors' Day, a special day for people to pay their respects to the elderly and a day for the elderly to enjoy themselves in China. As nine is the highest odd digit, two nines are taken to signify longevity.

From the above, we know the Chinese are fascinated with numbers. They celebrate all the doubled odd-numbered days as their holidays, such as the 1st of the first month the Spring Festival; the 3rd of the third month Shangsi Day (a day to clean oneself in the river); the 5th of the fifth moon the Dragon Boat Festival; the 7th of the seventh moon the Seventh Eve and the 9th of the ninth moon the Double Ninth Day. To the Chinese, even numbers are associative with Yin and odd numbers with the Yang (According to the Chinese Yin-yang theory, the cosmos is composed of the two opposing forces: the Yin which presents the feminine and negative force while the Yang masculine and positive).

The Chinese Language

甲骨文 *Oracle Bone Inscription*

The Chinese writing system, invented almost 5,000 years ago by a legendary person called Cang Jie differs greatly from the spellings of most other languages. Its formation is primarily based on pictographs or ideograms, representing each word by the physical appearance of the object. For example, tree 木, horse 馬, moon ☽, sheep 羊, mountain 山. As for words that do not have shape, such as actions, feelings, senses etc., the Chinese were creative enough to combine the created ideograms as the components to express them. For example, to denote "morning" the Chinese use the symbol "sun" with a horizontal line beneath the sun 旦 to express the time; and they combined "sun" and "moon" together to make the word 明 "bright". Nowadays, more than 90% of the Chinese characters in common use are made this way. For example, two 木 "trees" form 林 "woods"; three 木 "trees"form 森 "forest"; two 火 "fire"makes 炎 "heat". In addition,the different components carry different functions:the semantic component, called a radical, gives a clue to the meaning while the phonetic component gives a clue to pronunciation. For example, you will find there are two ways to write the Chinese characters: the classic way and the simplified way. The former one is in use in Taiwan, Hong Kong, Macao and other overseas Chinese communities while the latter one is used in mainland China, Singapore and Malaysia. To make the characters simpler and easier to write and remember, some most frequently used simplified characters were officially published in mainland China in 1964. There are totally 2,235 simplified characters contained in the "Simplified Character Table" published in 1964 by the Chinese government, so the majority of the Chinese characters are the same in the two forms, though the count of commonly-used Chinese characters is only about 3,500.

The Chinese adopted the "pinyin" system using the Roman alphabet to mark the pronunciations based on the northern dialect called Mandarin. Yet many areas in China still do not use pinyin signs which will make some difficulties for foreign visitors if they do not know some Chinese characters. Another fact is that there are still areas that people speak their own dialects instead of Mandarin. There are eight major dialects spoken in

China, such as Cantonese spoken in the southern part including Hong Kong and Macao, and Shanghainese spoken in Shanghai and its surrounding areas. The dialects usually differ greatly and are unintelligible.

What further annoys the foreign learners and visitors is that the Chinese language is a tonal language, which has four tones. The difference in intonation is the deciding factor in the meaning of the word. For example, "ma" with its first tone means "mother (妈)"; the second tone "to tingle (麻)"; the third tone "horse (马)" and the fourth tone "to curse (骂)". To make things worse, the same sound may have different characters with different meanings. For example, "han" with the fourth tone can mean "sweat (汗)", "the Chinese (汉)", "bravery (悍)" and "drought (旱)" etc.

The Chinese characters are living fossils, which represent how the Chinese interpret things and their relations with them. So we recommend anyone who wants to work and live in China learns the characters not just the pinyin because the characters serve more than a language to communicate with.

杯子 bēizi Cup
被子 bèizi Quilt

☺ *The Chinese language has four tones – ⁄ ∨ ＼.*
The difference in intonation is the deciding factor
in the meaning of the word.

Chinese Calligraphy

From right to left: 游天下江山第一楼

(Visit the world's No.1 building)

Chinese calligraphy, developed with the invention of the Chinese characters and becoming mature during the Han Dynasty (206 BC-AD 230), is regarded more than handwriting itself. It has traditionally been valued as the highest form of visual art. According to traditional Chinese philosophic thinking the truth and beauty cannot be exposed directly but rather represented with implications. The calligraphy just carries the manifestation of the philosophic idea. Each brush stroke in writing is infused with vital energy which animates the things and the ideas the words denote, such as the strokes of "rolling waves", "dewdrop about to fall", "startled snake slithering off into the grass" etc. The aesthetic images conveyed by the strokes are just like paintings but demand more imagination since the meanings are implicitly expressed rather than explicitly expressed in paintings.

Calligraphy is traditionally regarded as a form of self-cultivation and self-expression. Children are trained at an early age to practice writing. And people are often judged by their handwritings, for the Chinese think the force one used in writing betrays his dispositions, and the characters written reveal the calligrapher's understanding of the universe.

Good works of calligraphy can be found virtually everywhere in temples, on the sides of mountains and monuments as well as on the walls of sitting rooms. The tools to practice calligraphy are brush, ink, paper and ink-stone (where ink is mixed). They are called as the "four treasures of a scholar's study".

There are books and VCDs available in bookstores showing people how to practice calligraphy, and there are books of rubbings for you to follow some well-known calligraphers.

Calligraphy is also regarded as an active way of keeping fit and healthy, for the devotion to the practice is just like meditation to achieve relaxation and self-entertaining effects.

Four treasures of a
scholar's study
(文房四宝 wénfáng
sìbǎo)

brush (毛)笔 (máo) bǐ
ink 墨 mò
paper 纸 zhǐ
ink-stone 砚 yàn

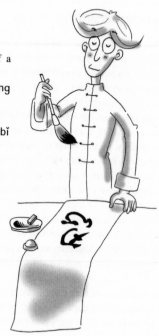

Chinese Painting

Contrary to the Western painting, which puts much emphasis on perspective, proportion and colour, Chinese painting demands more imagination when the onlooker looks at it. What the Chinese artists strive for is the concord between his feelings and the nature. To them the artistic beauty lies more often in portraying his personality in the nature, than in the perfection of proportion, build, and colouring. What the artist tries to portray is how the nature inspires him. The best painting to our Chinese eyes is not those, which resemble the real world, but the inner feelings of the artist in a natural rather than a dramatic way. So the tone of the artist seems detached rather than involved in the painting. And his love of nature is based upon a desire to identify his mind with nature and to enjoy nature as she is.

The main subject matters portrayed in traditional Chinese painting are landscape (literally "mountain and stream"), grass and flowers or birds and animals, which show how the traditional Chinese interpret the relationship between humans and the nature. Of course, there is also figure painting.

There are two major types of the Chinese painting in terms of style and skills: heavy-colored paintings done with fine delicate strokes and free-style ink and wash paintings. The former style was prevalent before the 12th century while the latter one popular afterwards. Later there are some artists combining the two together and form a hybrid of the two, i.e. semi fine stroke and semi free style.

Remember when you view a traditional Chinese painting not to neglect the poem and seals, which are always the integral parts of a fine painting. To the Chinese the calligraphy and the painting are of the same essence. Even the materials used in painting and calligraphy are almost identical.

Traditional
Chinese
Landscape
Painting

Chinese Houses

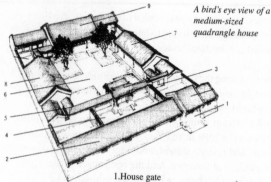

A bird's eye view of a medium-sized quadrangle house

1. House gate
2. Rooms sitting on the south and opening to the north (always serve as the study and reception room)
3. Screen
4. Outer courtyard
5. Circular corridor
6. Inner courtyard
7. Eastern wing rooms
8. Western wing rooms
9. Main rooms

Chinese people had a long settled life with their dwellings from primitive cave living to late sophisticated houses of special architectural styles.

The first thing the Chinese take into consideration before building their dwellings is the site. The common wisdom is to build the dwellings leaning against U-shaped hills with a stream running at the southwest side. The tall trees on the hills at the back of the houses withstand winds and restore waters, and are believed to restrain the outflow of fortunes. And the open space in the front facing the south helps to receive the sunlight to keep the houses warm and kill the harmful bacteria for sanitary reasons. The stream nearby facilitates the life with drinking water and washing.

The typical structure of the houses is an enclosed-walled building with the main hall on a south-north axis and the east- and west- winged living quarters on both sides of the hall. For big houses, there are three or five main halls with open spaces in between and the winged rooms at both sides connect the whole structure. The open space called Tianjing (literally means sky well) between the halls helps the house get enough sunlight and ventilation. The four-sided high walls protect the self-contained inside from the outside world. The typical representative residential buildings in the north are the quadrangles with a courtyard in the middle and houses on the four sides.

The walled structure, as a manifestation of the agrarian society, demonstrates the traditional Chinese lifestyle: self-contained with no adventurous spirit; interested in self-cultivation and perfection, and introverted with no public life.

Feng Shui

Feng Shui, literally meaning "wind and water," developing from very ancient times, is the study of the "built" environment. It is primarily focused on the Qi (cosmic energies) within a structure, as that is what has the most direct effect on the people. In another word, it is about aligning energies in living or working environment in a way that is most conducive with one's own personal energy. When it comes to the outside environment, the main points of concern is that the landscaping is beautiful and in balance with the rest of the environment. Feng Shui in the old days was known as "Kan Yu" (the observation of the forces between Heaven and Earth). Only towards the end of the Qing Dynasty did the term "Feng Shui" comes to be used unanimously to represent "Kan Yu". Feng Shui today is seen as interior design and house decorating,etc.

The foundation theory for Feng Shui is the five-element theory. They are: Wood(木 mù), Fire(火 huǒ), Earth(土 tǔ), Metal(金 jīn), and Water(水 shuǐ). These five elements interplay and form cyclical changes.

"Wood produces fire, fire produces earth, earth produces metal, metal produces water, water produces wood." They would also generate destructive effects. "Wood uproots earth, earth blocks water, water douses fire, fire melts metal, and metal chops wood". (Wood is green, fire is red, earth is yellow, metal is white or gold, and water is blue or black.) So the optimum combination of the five elements is of great importance.

Generating	Suppressing
Wood - Fire	Wood - Earth
Fire - Earth	Earth - Water
Earth - Metal	Water - Fire
Metal - Water	Fire - Metal
Water - Wood	Metal - Wood

For example, a plant (wood) grows when it is given water. When burnt, wood gives birth to fire, and the burnt ashes subsequently return to the earth.

The goal of Feng Shui is to create a comfortable and beautiful environment. And the key stress is to achieve balance.

Traditional Chinese Medicine

Traditional Chinese medicine, which has developed for some 5,000 years, works on different principles from the western medicine. The first difference is that the Chinese practitioners of medicine take a holistic approach while diagnosing the sick. They will take the whole body of the sick, his/her diet, age, habits, emotions, life-style and living environment etc. into consideration. They pay particular attention to the causes of the sickness instead of the sick part of the body. In another word, the approach is not symptomatic. So surgery to remove the symptoms is not encouraged in the Chinese medicine. Instead, in the traditional Chinese medicine, the cause of sickness results from the imbalance and blockage of the flow of " 气 qì", a vital force or energy which is instrumental for the workings of the human body and mind.(Qi flows in 12 channels (meridians) of energy, which correspond to 12 organs, and processes of the body). Treatment focuses on building up a profile of the sick and stresses impact on the Qi. There are many ways through which imbalances in Qi can be corrected. This includes acupuncture, herbal medicine, massage, diets and corrective and breathing exercises such as Tai Ji or Qi Gong.

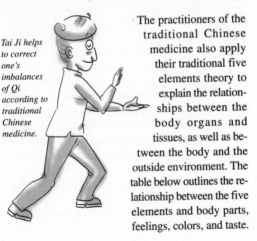

Tai Ji helps to correct one's imbalances of Qi according to traditional Chinese medicine.

The practitioners of the traditional Chinese medicine also apply their traditional five elements theory to explain the relationships between the body organs and tissues, as well as between the body and the outside environment. The table below outlines the relationship between the five elements and body parts, feelings, colors, and taste.

Element	Yin	Yang	Feelings	Colors	Tastes
Wood	Liver	Gall Bladder	Rage	Green	Sour
Fire	Heart	Small Intestine	Happiness	Red	Bitter
Earth	Spleen	Stomach	Thought	Yellow	Sweet
Metal	Lungs	Large Intestine	Sorrow	White	Spicy
Water	Kidneys	Bladder	Fear	Black	Salty

Another difference from the western medicine is that the traditional Chinese medicine places more emphasis on the prevention of illness rather than cure. So balanced diet, enough exercise and rest as well as regular lifestyle is the common prescriptions by the Chinese doctors.

To prevent sickness, the Chinese people are obsessed with eating tonics. Examples are abundant: ginseng, edible bird nests, the stag's horns, bear's paw, preserved longan and lichee, to name a few.

Auspicious Designs and Lucky Signs

Auspicious signs and patterns, expressing people's wishes for happiness and exorcising evil spirits, though pertaining to totem worship, enjoy a never-fading popularity among the Chinese people throughout the Chinese civilization.

The themes of auspicious designs range from imagery of people, animals, flowers, birds and wares to the Chinese characters, proverbs, benedictions and fairy tales. These designs are commonly expressed with metaphors, analogies, puns, symbols, and euphonies, etc.

Dragons, phoenixes, turtles, unicorns, lions, white cranes, magpies and mandarin ducks are thought to be auspicious and benevolent. The dragon-phoenix designs, the expressions as "Dragon and Phoenix Bringing Prosperity", "Two Dragons Playing with a Pearl", "Flying Dragon and Dancing Phoenix" and "A Couple of Phoenix Singing in Harmony", symbolizing prosperity and happiness, are common subject matter of artists. The signs with the two im-

龙凤呈祥 *lóng fèng chéng xiáng*
Dragon and Phoenix Bringing Prosperity

aged animals (The dragon the symbol of Yang and the phoe-nix the symbol of Yin) are often seen at weddings to indi-cate a harmonious marriage.

The lion, often seen in pairs flanking a palace gate or a garden gate, is also an auspicious animal. Made of bronze or stone, the male lion squats on the left, with one of its front legs stepping on a ball, and the female on the right stroking a cub. The former symbolizes power, unification and universality, and the latter fertility. The lions are re-garded as a divine guarding animal to drive away evil forces.

The turtle and white crane, which are thought can live for many years, are symbols of longevity. The picture "Pines and Red-crowned Cranes for Everlasting Spring" is the most widely accepted artistic form and gift for happiness. At a birthday ceremony for an elderly, you will find signs of these two animals. And the gifts to the elderly always include these designs.

松鹤延年 *sōng hè yán nián*
Pines and Red-crowned Cranes for
Everlasting Spring

The pine tree, bamboo and plum blossoms, jointly known as "three durable friends of winter," indicating people's unyielding and defiant characteristics are the favored subjects of the painters.

Lotus flower, with its "emerging unstained and uncontaminated from the filth", is the metaphor to honesty and incorruptibility, the desirable quality for the officials. This pattern of lotus is found embroidered on the official uniforms of the first-rank officials in Qing Dynasty. In the Chinese language, lotus (pronounced as "lian") is the homonym to incorruptibility.

The pattern with "an elephant carrying a vase" is seen in front of the emperor's throne in the Forbidden City's Hall of Supreme Harmony and on both sides of a path known as "Sacred Way", which leads to the emperors' tombs of the Ming and Qing dynasties. This auspicious motif is known as "Peace and prosperity accompany the elephant" or, simply, "Treasured elephant." Elephant (pronounced "xiang") is a homonym to "prosperity". Vase (pronounced "ping") is a homonym to "peace".

To express "peace in every season", the traditional design shows a vase with plum blossoms, narcissus, camellia, lily and orchid because these flowers bloom alternately in every season. They have been ascribed to different qualities by scholars and are most often seen in vases in China.

Similarly, to express "peace from year to year", the usual pattern is represented with a vase holding pine branches and plum blossoms, and firecrackers placed next to the vase. The pine branches indicates greenery in all seasons; plum blossoms are the only flowers to bloom in the winter; and the firecrackers, which are set off during the Spring Festival, are meant to ward off evils. Setting off firecrackers during the Spring Festival is an old folk custom. Before gunpowder was invented, people set fire to bamboo at celebrations. Since bamboo cracks when it burns, so we get the name "firecrackers." This "cracking of burning bamboo" is a homonym of "year" (Both are pronounced "sui"). The more bamboo stalks there are, the more broken bamboo pieces there will be; thus, we have the auspicious saying, "peace from year to year".

The image of "bat" is another auspicious sign very commonly seen throughout every corner in China. The bat, pronounced as "fu" is homonym to "fortune".

The auspicious signs and patterns are so pervasive, and the ways to illustrate the yearnings and desires are very unique to expose the Chinese imagination and thinking.

Appendix

Learn the following useful Chinese expressions from the CD:

GREETINGS AND INTRODUCTIONS

Have You Eaten?

Here are some common Chinese greetings:

Have you eaten? 吃过饭了吗？ (Chīguo fàn le ma?)

Yes(I have). 吃过了。 (Chīguo le.)

Are you busy recently? 最近忙吗？ (Zuìjìn máng ma?)

Yes, quite busy. 挺忙的。 (Tǐng máng de.)

Where are you going? 去哪儿啊？ (Qù nǎr a?)

Oh, just have a walk. 走走。 (Zǒuzou.)

You are waiting for the bus? 在等车啊？ (Zài děngchē a?)

Yes. 是的。 (Shìde.)

You are reading the book? 在看书啊？ (Zài kànshū a?)

Yes. 嗯。 (Ng.)

You are back? 回来了？ (Huílái le?)

You are going out? 出去啊？ (Chūqu a?)

Hello and Happiness

Here are some expressions about Chinese names:

What's your name? 你叫什么名字？

(Nǐ jiào shénme míngzi?)

My name is... 我叫…… (Wǒ jiào...)

What's your surname? 你姓什么？ / 您贵姓？

(Nǐ xìng shénme? / Nín guì xìng?)

My surname is ... 我姓…… (Wǒ xìng ...)

Using "Ni Hao"

Here are more greeting expressions under different occasions:

Hello, Manager. 经理好！ (Jīnglǐ hǎo !)

Hello, Director. 主任好！ (Zhǔrèn hǎo !)

Have you got a cold? 你感冒了吗？

(Nǐ gǎnmào le ma?)

Have you put on enough clothes?

你衣服穿够了吗？ (Nǐ yīfu chuān gòu le ma?)

You should drink more hot water.

你要多喝点开水。 (Nǐ yào duō hē diǎn kāishuǐ.)

"What's Your Sign?"

The 12 animal signs:

十二生肖（shí'èr shēngxiào）：

Rat 鼠(shǔ)	Ox 牛(niú)	Tiger 虎(hǔ)
Rabbit 兔(tù)	Dragon 龙(lóng)	Snake 蛇(shé)
Horse 马(mǎ)	Sheep 羊(yáng)	Monkey 猴(hóu)
Rooster 鸡(jī)	Dog 狗(gǒu)	Pig 猪(zhū)

Discussion of animal signs is a favorite topic among the Chinese.

What's your animal sign? 你属什么(Nǐ shǔ shénme？)
I am... 我属……(Wǒ shǔ...)

GETTING ALONG WITH CHINESE ETIQUETTE

In the Home

Host: Well, sorry, there aren't many dishes. Please help yourself.

主人：不好意思，没什么菜。请随便吃。

(Zhǔrén: Bù hǎoyìsi, méi shénme cài. Qǐng suíbiàn chī.)

Guest: Oh, there are so many dishes here and hardly can we finish them.

客人：哪里哪里，这么多菜，吃不完的。

116

(Kèrén: Nǎli nǎli, zhème duō cài, chī bù wán de.)

Table Manners

It's delicious. 好吃！（Hǎochī！）

Thank you. The dishes you cooked are so delicious.

谢谢！你做的菜真好吃！

（Xièxie！Nǐ zuòde cài zhēn hǎochī！）

In a Restaurant

Please give me the menu. 请给我菜单。

（Qǐng gěi wǒ càidān.）

It's on my treat this time. 这次我请客！

（Zhècì wǒ qǐngkè！）

I'll pay next time.下次我请客！（Xiàcì wǒ qǐngkè！）

Cheers. 干杯！（Gānbēi！）

Eating is Heaven

Well-known Chinese sayings about eating:

Eating is heaven. 民以食为天。(Mín yǐ shí wéi tiān.)

Food and sex are the natural desires of human beings.

食色，性也。(Shí sè, xìng yě.)

The beauty and elegance can serve as food.

秀色可餐。(Xiùsè kě cān.)

The skills to run a country are like those to bake a small fish (Both need precaution and patience).

治大国如烹小鲜。(Zhì dàguó rú pēng xiǎoxiān.)

The Color Red

In China, the red color is always associated with "happiness and good fortune".

Red 红色(hóngsè)

Yellow resembles the color of earth and soil and it used to be the exclusive color used by the Emperors in China.

Yellow 黄色(huángsè)

Green represents life and vitality, while black and white are associated with death.

Green 绿色(lùsè) Black 黑色(hēisè)

White 白色(báisè)

The Great Harmonious World

The Chinese tend to seek the common grounds between each other while avoiding direct confrontation. There is abundance of the Chinese idioms reflecting this philosophic thinking.

Harmony is what matters.

和为贵 (Hé wéi guì.)

To live harmoniously between each other.

和平共处 (Hépíng gòngchǔ.)

Harmony will lead to wealth and fortune.

和气生财 (Héqì shēng cái.)

Golden mean. 中庸之道 (Zhōng yōng zhī dào.)

One Promise is Worth a Thousand Bars of Gold

One promise is worth a thousand bars of gold.

一诺千金 (yí nuò qiān jīn)

What is said can't be unsaid. (A word once spoken cannot be overtaken even by a team of four horses)

一(yì one)言(yán word)既出(jìchū come out), 驷马(sìmǎ a team of four horses)难(nán difficult)追(zhuī chase)

Interesting Numbers

One 一(yī) Two 二(èr) Three 三(sān) Four 四(sì)

Five 五(wǔ) Six 六(liù) Seven 七(qī) Eight 八(bā)

Nine 九(jiǔ) Ten 十(shí) Hundred 百(bǎi)

Thousand 千(qiān) Ten thousand 万(wàn)

Some common auspicious expressions associated with numbers:

For 1: Heart and soul; wholeheartedly.

一(yì one)心(xīn heart)一(yí one)意(yì soul)

For 2: Auspicious things always come in pairs.

好事(hǎoshì auspicious things)成双(chéngshuāng in pairs)

For 4: Wish you good fortune in all four seasons.

四季(sìjì four seasons)发财(fācái make a fortune)

For 5: Abundant harvest of all food crops.

五谷(wǔgǔ five crops)丰登(fēngdēng harvest)

For 6: May everything go smoothly.

六六(liùliù six and six)大顺(dàshùn smoothly)

For 9: Enduring as heaven and earth; everlasting and unchanging.(nine, a homonym of the word forever)

天(tiān sky)长(cháng everlasting)地(dì earth)久(jiǔ forever)

For 10: Be perfect in everyway.

十(shí ten)全(quán complete)十(shí ten)美(měi beautiful)

For 10,000: May everything go as you wish.

万事(wànshì literally ten thousand things)如意(rúyì according to your wish)

Giving Gifts

The gift is trifling but the sentiment is profound.

礼轻情意重。 (Lǐ qīng qíngyì zhòng.)

Understanding Chinese Girls

A white complexion is powerful enough to hide three faults.

一白(yì bái　a white complexion)遮(zhē hide)三(sān three)丑(chǒu ugly)

Where? Where?

When walking in the company of three, there must be one I can learn from. (by Confucious)

三人行，必有我师焉。 —— 孔子

(Sān rén xíng, bì yǒu wǒ shī yān. —— Kǒngzǐ)

Modesty helps one move forward, whereas conceit makes one lag behind. (by Mao Zedong)

虚心使人进步，骄傲使人落后。 —— 毛泽东

(Xūxīn shǐ rén jìnbù, jiāo'ào shǐ rén luòhòu.

—— Máo Zédōng)

CHINESE TRADITIONS AND CULTURE

Spring Festival

Learn some useful words and expressions for the biggest

festival in China.

Wish a Happy New Year. Send New Year greetings.

拜年 (bài nián)

Spring Festival 春节 (Chūnjié)

the last day of the last month of the lunar year

大年三十 (dà nián sān shí)

the first day of the first month of the lunar year

正月初一 (zhēng yuè chū yī)

Spring Festival couplets 春联 (chūnlián)

firecrackers 鞭炮 (biānpào)

lucky money for Spring Festival 压岁钱 (yāsuìqián)

red envelope 红包 (hóngbāo)

Special foods for this festival include:

饺子 (jiǎozi) a kind of dumpling

年糕 (niángāo)

a kind of cake made of ground glutinous rice eaten in the festival

八宝粥 (bābǎozhōu)

a special porridge with eight ingredients of grains or rice

Dragon Boat Festival

Dragon Boat Festival 端午节 (Duānwǔ jié)

the fifth day of the fifth month of the lunar calendar

五月初五 (wǔ yuè chū wǔ)

Dragon Boat Racing Competition

赛龙舟 (sài lóngzhōu)

Special food for this festival is:

粽子 (zòngzi) dumpling made of glutinous rice wrapped in bamboo or reed leaves

Mid-Autumn Festival

Mid-Autumn Festival 中秋节 (Zhōngqiū jié)

Mooncake 月饼 (yuèbing)

Learn a well-known poem about this festival:

I raise my head, the splendid moon I see;

Then droop my head, and sink to dreams of my hometown.

By Li Bai (famous poet in Tang Dynasty)

举头望明月，低头思故乡——李白

(Jǔtóu wàng míngyuè, dītóu sī gùxiāng.

—— Lǐ Bái)

Lantern Festival

Lantern Festival 元宵节 (Yuánxiāo jié)

Dragon lantern 龙灯 (lóngdēng)

walking on stilts 踩高跷 (cǎi gāoqiāo)

Special food for this festival is:

元宵 (yuánxiāo), also called 汤圆 (tāngyuán), a kind of special round dumplings

Qing Ming (Tomb-Sweeping Day)

Tomb-Sweeping Day 清明节 (Qīngmíng jié)

sweep tomb 扫墓 (sǎomù)

Tree leaves will eventually return to their root.

叶落归根 (Yè luò guī gēn.)

Learn a well-known poem about this festival:

It drizzles endlessly during the rainy season in spring,
Travelers along the road look gloomy and miserable.

By Du Mu (famous poet in Tang Dynasty)

清明时节雨纷纷，路上行人欲断魂。——杜牧

(Qīngmíng shíjié yǔ fēnfēn, lùshang xíngrén yù duànhún.

—— Dù Mù)

The Double Ninth Holiday

Double Ninth Holiday 重阳节 (Chóngyáng jié)

Learn a well-known poem about this festival:

All alone in a foreign land, I am twice as homesick on this day.
When brothers carry dogwood up the mountain,
Each of them a branch and my branch missing.

By Wang Wei (famous poet in Tang Dynasty)

独在异乡为异客，每逢佳节倍思亲。遥知兄弟登高
处，遍插茱萸少一人。——王维

(Dú zài yìxiāng wéi yìkè, měi féng jiājié bèi sīqīn.
Yáo zhī xiōngdì dēng gāochù, biàn chā zhūyú shǎo
yì rén.

—— Wáng Wéi)

Chinese Calligraphy
calligraphy 书法 (shūfǎ)
One's handwriting always betrays one's personality.
字如其人 (zì rú qí rén)
four treasures of a scholar's study
文房四宝 (wénfáng sìbǎo)
brush 笔 (bǐ)
ink 墨 (mò)
paper 纸 (zhǐ)
ink stone 砚 (yàn)